T0194603

# KINGDOM
## WARRIOR MEN'S
# DEVOTIONAL

## DOUGLAS DICKERSON

authorHOUSE®

AuthorHouse™
1663 Liberty Drive
Bloomington, IN 47403
www.authorhouse.com
Phone: 1 (800) 839-8640

© 2019 Douglas Dickerson. All rights reserved.

No part of this book may be reproduced, stored in a retrieval system, or transmitted by any means without the written permission of the author.

Scripture taken from the New King James Version®. Copyright © 1982 by Thomas Nelson. Used by permission. All rights reserved.

Published by AuthorHouse 02/23/2019

ISBN: 978-1-7283-0190-7 (sc)
ISBN: 978-1-7283-0189-1 (e)

Print information available on the last page.

Any people depicted in stock imagery provided by Getty Images are models, and such images are being used for illustrative purposes only. Certain stock imagery © Getty Images.

This book is printed on acid-free paper.

Because of the dynamic nature of the Internet, any web addresses or links contained in this book may have changed since publication and may no longer be valid. The views expressed in this work are solely those of the author and do not necessarily reflect the views of the publisher, and the publisher hereby disclaims any responsibility for them.

# INTRODUCTION

*Blessed be the Lord my Rock and my great strength, who
trains my hands for war and my fingers for battle.*
—Psalm 144:1

King David was one of the greatest warriors in the Bible and he
was a pretty good worshiper on a harp. True warfare and worship
are inseparable. How can you and I be true worshipers of God and
not be moved to action by the evil of our time and to set other men
free? King David understood God as a "Man of war" (Exodus 15:3).
So, God is a warrior, and He uses the title "Lord of hosts" or "Lord
of armies" ten times more than all His other titles. That was not by
accident! This is a time for war! There can be no victory without
a battle. The measure of victory depends on the measure of the
battle. There has been a very crafty mentality invading over much
of the church—namely, that you and I, as Christian men, should
not experience troubles, and if we do, we are not walking in faith.
For that reason, this men's devotional and journal was written. It
was said of the ministry of the Apostle Paul that this kingdom
warrior went about "strengthening and establishing" the hearts of

the disciples encouraging them to remain firm in the faith, saying, "It is through many tribulations and hardships that we must enter the kingdom of God" (Acts 14:22). We must not fall for the trap of the enemy in trying to use carnal weapons (2 Corinthians 10:3–6). When Christian warriors tried to conquer with carnal weapons, it resulted in some of the worst atrocities ever known to mankind. For that reason, this men's devotional and journal was written. Warriors who are ignorant of our own history often repeat the same mistakes. The kingdom of the God will not come by might or power but by the Spirit (Zechariah 4:6)! As we'll see in these pages, all these accounts have been recorded in the Bible to inspire, teach, warn, and model how to live—and how not to live. It is my prayer as you read the devotionals in this book, you'll get to know God at a deeper level and see yourself as a "kingdom warrior." As you spend your devotion time with God, take a few minutes to read the true stories of warriors in this devotional and the battle plans that follow. Think about the context of each warrior's life and the role he played in God's kingdom plans. Then journal your thoughts and insights using the scriptures as your guide in the battle plan. As you pray, ask yourself, "What has this warrior's life taught me about my own place in God's kingdom plans?" You won't regret it! You will learn more than you expect about God and how He desires to interact with you as a warrior—a "kingdom warrior." That only happens if we really know God and are made strong in Him. Then we also shall do great exploits (Daniel 11:32).

# KINGDOM WARS

Prepare for war! Wake up mighty men, let all the men of war draw
near, let them come up. Beat your plowshares into swords and
your pruning hooks into spears; let the weak say "I am Strong."
—Joel 3:9–10

True leadership is always of a new breed. This is because following
old paths is not leading; it is following. The prophet Joel improvised
in battle using farming tools. He calls farmers to fashion their tools
into weapons of war. He invented a different way of fighting. Joel
is one of the great examples of a new breed of warriors. It could be
said of Joel that even when he was a prophet he carried himself like
a warrior. Although he always saw himself as a kingdom warrior, he
could have been frustrated as a man of his ability. He didn't waste
away in bitterness; he just kept "preparing" for the day he would
be needed. Every war has a cause. The battle is in the spiritual
dimension yet fought both on earth and in the heavens. Our combat
is against spiritual forces—not men. Demonic enemies are behind
much of what comes against our marriages, families, and churches.
Your faith in the Word of God equips you to maintain a "battle

stance" against the enemy. Joel looked forward to a time when the Lord would bring judgment to the enemies of God and of Israel, when the nations would be called to give account for their actions. In the natural world, we cannot see or participate in this conflict of good versus evil. But God, even though He could win on His own, has chosen us as His kingdom warriors. A new age is born, men in the church are empowered, and now "let the weak say, 'I am strong!'"

## Battle Plan

Don't waste your time. Protect the ground taken from the enemy. Stand in readiness for a counterattack. Keep your ground (Psalms 60:9–12; 144:1–8; Ephesians 6:10–18).

# THE CALLING OF GOD

Then Samson called to the Lord, saying, "O Lord God ..."
—Judges 16:28

The fulfillment of every goal requires preparation, usually in the form of training, exercise, and practice. God is pursuing His sons. The Spirit of the Lord is calling us to war. The call causes us to go to war. His roar causes us to draw near to Him and to each other. We must manifest on the earth what God says in heaven. The more significant the goal, the more planning is required. The ability to plan is a rare skill, but few ever accomplish anything without it. Our ability to do anything for God is not really ours at all; it is His ability at work in us. How we need to learn a lesson from Samson! When we first hear his name, we tend to think of a stereotype: the strong man with long hair, a perfect physique, and a brilliant mind. However, there is no indication in the Word of God that Samson looked much different from any other man in his generation. God does not play favorites. Everyone can embrace this call to become a kingdom warrior. If we believe in Jesus, we are automatically enlisted in His army. Samson was undefeated—but not invincible. His constant disobedience led him to compromise the covenant he had with God. Samson's strength was not his muscles, his mind, or his family name. It wasn't even his long hair. His strength was in the covenant of dedication he made to God, and his mighty acts were a result of the Holy Ghost moving upon him in power. Samson could rend lions and conquer Philistines, but he could not rend his lust or conquer his appetites. Woe to those who feel they can do God's work in their own strength! The same is true today. Men must come to the place where they recognize it is all of Him and none of them. We cannot depend on ourselves! It is just us: carpenters, bus drivers, custodians, farmers, and the like. Men of common stock fill the ranks in God's army of warriors. God calls us from our everyday lives to be separated out and holy unto Him!

## Battle Plan

The Lord will always hear a prayer of humility. Have no fellowship with the world (Romans 6:13; 1 Peter 5:8; 1 John 2:15–17).

# THE POWER OF MOVING

And he believed in the Lord, and God
accounted it to him for righteousness.
—Genesis 15:6

At the starting line of a new year, people with good intentions define their goals in order to be successful. Knowing your goal can help, but that alone is not enough. Before we know it, December comes as we struggle to achieve our purpose. Why? Because we failed to stay focused on our goal in faith. Abraham is the father of faith and the faithful. From this "friend of God" (James 2:23), we learn that faith is not perfect character or integrity. Rather, it is simply taking God at His word. Abraham's life speaks to us about how we benefit from believing what God says despite evidence to the contrary. In the biblical account of creation, the Holy Spirit was moving. Nothing happens for those who sit and dream. Water that is not moving becomes stagnant very quickly. The same is true of human life. To keep moving requires a willingness to leave comfort and security behind. We must not become addicted to our comfort zones. Faith is spelled R-I-S-K. Like Abraham, learn to be secure and bold in the place of risk. Staying where you are is not an option. Staying where you are is a worse prison than suffering another defeat. Those who do not suffer defeats are those who are not in the fight. If you are not in the fight of life, you are no longer alive but just exist. If you try to go forward, you may get hurt again—but that is not the worst thing that can happen to you. The worst thing of all is to pass out of this life knowing that you did not accomplish what you could have. Have courage, you mighty man! Regardless of their present situation, kingdom warriors always find a way out. That's you and me! The door can be found only by those who live by faith—R-I-S-K. Are you ready?

**Battle Plan**

Courage is not the absence of fear; it is the action not to let fear control what you do. The road to success is marked for warriors who see with the eyes of courage (Genesis 22:1–19; Romans 4:9–12; Hebrews 11:8–12).

# THE FIRST KINGDOM
# WAR ON EARTH

Then the man said, "The women whom You gave to
be with me, she gave me of the tree, and I ate."
—Genesis 3:12

Imagine walking, talking, and communing with the Spirit of God all day long. That is how it was with this kingdom man, Adam, in the garden. This perfect communion caused the garden to prosper. This was God's ultimate plan. But Adam left the true plan of communion and disobeyed God. We find that after the fall, communion becomes the biggest war between humankind and God. Hide and seek is our choice. Hiding is so contrary to what God wants us to do as kingdom men. He prefers that we come before Him boldly and that we walk and talk with Him. I am sure God is asking many of us today the same question He asked Adam, "Where are you?" (Genesis 3:9). Every failure seems to attract an excuse. Adam began making excuses for his willful disobedience. "Well ... it was the woman ... the woman You gave me, I might add. She gave me the fruit, and ... yeah, I guess I ate it. I'm only human!" Excuses! Excuses! Adam led the blame-shifting parade that so many of us men have marched in ever since. Kingdom warriors don't fault God and others for their own shortcomings. This separates the men from the boys. The foot soldiers from the kingdom warriors. Man fell by choice. Before then, Adam had communion and dominion. Now, he would sweat and toil. What would have happened if Adam had come clean and owned up to his failure? We'll never know. The far more relevant question is whether we will own up to ours.

**Battle Plan**

Don't challenge God's Word. Ask instead what God's Word means to you. How can you apply it to your life? Our opinions are easy prey to Satan's deception (Psalm 8; Romans 5:12–21; 1 John 2:15–17).

# OUR CHIEF WEAPON

*It is written; man shall not live by bread alone, but by
every word that proceeds from the mouth of God.*
—Matthew 4:4

A strong knowledge of the enemy's weapons, strategies, strength, and weaknesses can mean the difference between success and failure on the battlefield. The devil knows a lot about spiritual battle— especially about our weakness and faults as men. He enjoys using his kingdom to harass us, lie to us, and tempt us. Since he's been doing this for thousands of years, he has developed a twisted and evil art form. How can we fight the tactics of such an enemy? Matthew 4:1–11 gives us the perfect example. There, Jesus faced some very real temptations from His very real enemy. Right off the bat, the devil pounced on Jesus's most immediate weakness: hunger. You'd be hungry, too, after fasting for forty days! Satan wanted to derail the divine plan that Jesus had freely chosen to follow, so he offered this suggestion: "If you're really the Son of God, turn these rocks into bread." Jesus recognized the devil's tactics. Though Satan had unleashed his weapon, Jesus had one that was far more effective:

the Word of God. We too as men must wield the Word of God as a sword in times of need. With prayer, we engage in the battle and the purpose for which we are armed. To put on the armor of God is to be prepared for battle. Jesus versus Satan—there was no match. The battle ended before it began because the devil had no counterattacks strong enough to overcome the warrior Jesus, who used God's Word as His chief weapon.

## Battle Plan

When you use the word of God, you can never be defeated. Give yourself to faithful prayer (Psalm 33:6–9; Ephesians 6:17; Hebrews 4:12; 1 Peter 1:24–25).

# THE WARRIOR

For the Lord does not see as man sees; for man looks at the
outward appearance, but the Lord looks at the heart.
—1 Samuel 16:7

The spirit of the Lord accompanies the anointing of little David by
the prophet Samuel. From this moment, God begins to equip David
and direct the details of his life, although it will be some years before
he takes the throne. David is about fifteen years old at this time.
Imagine a conversation between God and Samuel: "I'm fashioning
a warrior," He said.

> "Oh Lord, he is too small!"
> "No," He said, "he is just the right size."
> "Lord, remember Samson?"
> "Yes, he was a real warrior."
> "Make him like that, Lord."
> "No this is my warrior. And his strength will be
> in Me."
> "Lord, his heart is too tender."
> "His heart is just right," He said.

"What weapon will he use?"

"The first one will be a harp."

"What kind of weapon is that?"

"A harp is strong weapon."

"What else, Lord? Perhaps a sword or a huge spear."

"He will use them later, but not yet."

"What other weapon then, Lord?"

"His voice," He said.

"Oh, a voice like Elijah's to call down fire upon his enemies."

"No, he will have the pleasant voice of a minstrel. With his voice, he will wield worship. And that is a strong weapon indeed."

"Where will you train this warrior, Lord?"

"The right place for this warrior is in the meadows."

"Lord, what kind of warrior is this—so small, tender heart, and unusual weapons? What enemy will this little one ever slay?"

"He will slay many. His enemies will not be small … There, I am done."

"Lord? Lord? He's just a boy, Lord!"

"Yes, he's a boy, and he will slay giants."

## Battle Plan

Do not judge based upon what you see. Do not overvalue size. God looks at the heart. Obedience will establish on your authority (1 Samuel 13:5–14; Psalm 89:19–23; Isaiah 66:1–2; Luke 18:9–14).

# A HEART FOR THE
# THRONE ROOM

O Lord, You have searched me and known me. You
know my sitting down and my rising up; You understand
my thought afar off. You comprehend my path and my
lying down, and are acquainted with all my ways.
—Psalm 139:1–3

Many men don't come into the Throne Room "boldly" because they
forget they are approaching a throne of grace. Let's be honest, we
think of the Throne Room as judgment. To come "boldly" means don't
be reserved and to come in with frankness and full-open speech. Our
King of kings and Lord of lords has big shoulders for every kingdom
warrior. We gain new grace and faith for our present circumstances.
King David had a heart for the Throne Room. In Psalm 139, he
expressed his intimate relationship with God and was consoled in
the truth that God is always and everywhere present. How did David
know these things? He knew God intimately through spending much
time with Him in the Throne Room! David had read about God in
His written Word, had learned his own need for God's forgiveness

and mercy, and had often enjoyed God's protection and blessing. The Throne Room is where God searches us, knows us, and tries us. It is the place where He finds no impurities or dross, has to be put in a refiner's crucible. Even though we are being tested, we must have access to the Throne Room to find the grace to endure. From this place, we rule with Him as kingdom warriors. Nothing shapes your life like an intimate, growing relationship with God.

**Battle Plan**

You must pray truthfully, and you need never fear an enemy at the throne of grace (Psalm 139; Romans 11:33–36; 1 Corinthians 2:13–16; Hebrews 4:14–16).

# FAITHFUL WARRIOR

Tychicus, a beloved brother, faithful minister, fellow
servant in the Lord, will tell you all the news about me.
—Colossians 4:7

It has been said there are three kinds of men in the world: those
who make things happen, those who watch things happen, and
those who wonder what's happening. A man in the Bible named
Tychicus was a leader who made things happen. The apostle Paul
commended him as a faithful and "beloved brother." Although the
name Tychicus means "chance happening," the Lord, not chance,
brought Tychicus into Paul's life. Tychicus lived up to the Marines'
motto: *Semper fidelis* (often shortened to Semper Fi), which means
"always faithful." Leaders are made from those who know what is
happening and are not content to sit on the sidelines of life and watch
others determine their affairs. They recognize opportunities and
seize them with boldness. They are the kingdom warriors who make
things happen. The faithfulness of Tychicus won Paul's confidence
that sent him to Crete, a difficult mission field (Titus 3:12). Only
a kingdom warrior could handle such a tough ministry assignment.

Even as Paul neared the time of his martyrdom, he sent Tychicus to Ephesus on a special mission (2 Timothy 4:12). You don't have to be a US Marine to live by the motto Semper Fi. You can be "always faithful" as a husband, father, brother, or coworker. Be honest: Does the term faithful describe you? Could you appear on the same list as Tychicus, the "faithful helper"?

## Battle Plan

Someone is counting on your faithfulness. Not one of us lives for himself (Psalm 101; Proverbs 20:6; Luke 16:10–13).

# A WARRIOR'S WITNESS

And the keeper of the prison, awaking from sleep and seeing
the prison doors open, supposing the prisoners had fled, drew
his sword and was about to kill himself. But Paul called with a
loud voice, saying, "Do yourself no harm, for we are all here."
—Acts 16:27–28

Everyone wants to see a cause-and-effect relationship between what
you say and how you live. That is especially true in the spiritual
context of a kingdom warrior. A jailer in the city of Philippi got a
close look at how real faith in Jesus affected two men. They were
both in jail for preaching about Jesus. Instead of sorrow, something
else rose up in the midst of that jail. As this jailer slept on the job, an
earthquake shook open all the prison doors and chains holding all the
prisoners, including Paul and Silas. The Lord delivered His servants
by means of a Holy Ghost jailbreak. Rather than die painfully at
the hands of the Romans, the jailer decided to take his own life.
Just then, he heard two of the prisoners imploring him not to harm
himself. The Philippian jailer knew immediately that Paul and Silas
had something that he wanted for himself. What a picture of grace!

The same man who had locked them up, who had participated in their beating, now desiring pardon from a God he discovered through their witness. A kingdom warrior's witness! "Sirs," he said, his voice probably trembling with relief, "what must I do to be saved?" (Acts 16:30). In an instant, the jailer was set free from a prison far greater than the one to which he kept the keys. As a husband, father, or coworker, is your life a beacon of God's joy and peace? People are watching us.

**Battle Plan**

Live a fully submitted life of obedience and trust in God. Praise triumphs gloriously!

(Acts 16:25–34; 1 Corinthians 9:19–23; 10:32–33; Galatians 5:13–15).

# ARE YOU ARMED WITH FAITH?

Jesus said to him, "If you can believe, all things are possible to
him who believes." Immediately the father of the child cried
out and said with tears, "Lord I believe; help my unbelief!"
—Mark 9:23–24

The faith we have will determine the course of our lives. It will be
a primary determining factor of whether we succeed or fail. History
testifies that there is no force on earth that can stop true faith. At
times, we need some assurance before we can take a leap of faith.
The unnamed father of a demon-possessed boy needed that kind of
assurance. Jesus fully intended to heal the boy, but first He dealt with
the man's doubts. "All things are possible to him who believes," He
told him, intending to build the man's faith. The question deciding
the issue is not Jesus's power but the man's faith. This desperate father
had no doubt heard about Jesus and the miracles He had performed,
but for some reason, he couldn't bring himself to fully believe that
Jesus could do what the disciples had tried to do. "Lord, I believe," he
told Jesus. "Help my unbelief!" Since faith is a gift, we may pray for it
as this father did. This father was a fighter and didn't give up on his

boy. He was a kingdom warrior for his son's healing. Men, wherever an atmosphere of unbelief makes it difficult to believe, we should seek a different setting. Prayer and praise provide an atmosphere of faith in God. What is the obstacle in your life, marriage, family, and work? If you want God to do great things in your life, you will need faith. Your faith in God is the key to your receiving.

**Battle Plan**

Don't be afraid to ask God to assure you and strengthen your faith. He is more than willing to do that! (Matthew 17:20; Mark 9:14–29; John 11:40; Romans 10:9; James 5:16)

# DON'T DROP YOUR GUARD

"Get up, sanctify the people. ... You cannot stand before your enemies until You take away the accursed thing from among you."
—Joshua 7:13

In these times, there seems to be an assault on every moral principle based on character. This attack on values can be the finest hour for the true warrior. Men with destiny and purpose can rise higher than ever because their light shines brighter in darkness. The failure to detect and deal with sin caused Israel's defeat at Ai. Our past successes can cause us to be less careful about sin. None of us can afford to drop our guard, for even one person's sins can weaken the life of a whole family, church, and nation. God will dress you for the battle you are living in. We cannot wear the Lord's anointing without hearing and obeying His voice clearly. Joshua listened to God and consecrated the people of Israel. This meant they needed to be morally clean. It also suggests that we are to be separated from the world around us. Our garments do not look the same as those in the world. You are free to do right or wrong, but you must also understand that your choice has consequences. We can be a slave and be free if our vision is greater than our chains. We can be free, wealthy, and powerful and still be a slave if our fears are greater than our vision. Fear is our most deadly enemy. For kingdom fighters, it is always right to fight for freedom. We cannot be who we were created to be (kingdom warriors) without freedom. Release the warrior in you! True Godly character is dependent not upon our environment but what is within us. What good is it to accomplish the greatest goals if you lose your Godly character in the process?

**Battle Plan**

The weapons you have for war are important. The first thing you have to do is not check your weapons but to check your heart (Zechariah 3:1–5; Romans 6:15–23; Colossians 2:11–12).

# FACING OPPOSITION

"What are these feeble Jews doing? Will they fortify
themselves? Will they offer sacrifices? Will they
complete it in a day? Will they revive the stones from
the heaps of rubbish—stones that are burned?"
—Nehemiah 4:2

When you're in the trenches of God's will, if you stick your head
up a little higher than anyone else to try to see you, you will be
shot at. If any man today tries to rise above the confines in which
everyone else is wasting away, they will quickly become the target of
jealous accusers and slanderers. Spiritual opposition often confirms
that you're headed in the right direction. Nehemiah endured this
kind of opposition as he worked to rebuild the ruined city walls
around Jerusalem. Much of that opposition came from a Samaritan
leader named Sanballat, a sworn enemy of the Jewish people who did
everything he could to stop Nehemiah's work. First, he mocked and
ridiculed the Jews. When that tactic failed, he turned to weapons
of fear and entrapment. Because Nehemiah was dedicated to God
and proceeded in his work with prayerful wisdom, Sanballat's

effort failed. The city grew in size, the walls were rebuilt, and the residents remained focused in seeing the task completed. In fact, they added weapons to their list of masonry tools. For every project God assigns you, expect a "Sanballat" to be working behind the scenes to discourage you. We too have an enemy who is doing all that he can to keep up pinned down in the trenches. It is a victory for him to keep us in deadlock. The main question is not whether opposition will appear but how you will respond when it arrives. Spiritual enemies are bent on opposing our efforts to be a godly husband and father and be godly influences on those around us. Don't give in! Why? "Our God will fight for us" (Nehemiah 4:20).

**Battle Plan**

Strengthen your sense of resolve. Ignore the reproaches and insults. Support those who are under spiritual attack (2 Chronicles 20:15–25; Psalm 109; Matthew 26:41; Hebrews 3:4).

# COMBATTING ENVY

Now Cain talked with Abel his brother; and it came
to pass, when they were in the field, that Cain rose
up against Abel his brother and killed him.
—Genesis 4:8

The Bible introduces us to the power of envy in the person of
Cain, who murdered his brother, Abel. When God accepted Abel's
sacrifice, Cain flew into a murderous rage. Cain didn't kill Abel on
a whim. He let feelings of envy and jealousy build up until he had
devised a scheme for taking the life of his brother, who had done
him no wrong. Cain asks, "Am I my brother's keeper?" (Genesis 4:9).
"Absolutely" is God's answer. The word used for "keeper" means "one
who guards and protects." Men, we are held accountable by God,
for our treatment to our brothers (blood and spiritual). However,
we find another disastrous pattern recorded in Genesis 4:16: "Then
Cain went out from the presence of the Lord." When we do not
worship the way the Lord wants us to, we begin to create our own
society. Cain and his entire family paid a heavy price for his envy.
Five generations later, we read that Lamech, a descendant of Cain,

kills a man (Genesis 4:23). When we are out from the presence of the Lord, sinful patterns go from generation to generation. It took Seth being born in order for proper fellowship and worship of God to be restored (Genesis 4:25–26). A little bit of Cain lives in every man. Think about the anger you feel when someone you believe is less qualified gets promoted ahead of you. That's envy! What about the jealousy over a business rival? That's envy at work! Kingdom warriors protect and guard each other. Learn to be content with what God has given you and where He has placed you. Men, "Let brotherly love continue" (Hebrews 13:1).

## Battle Plan

Combat envy by choosing to rejoice with others. Envy has no room to take root in the soil of genuine joy! (Romans 14:16–21; 1 Corinthians 8:9–13; Galatians 5:13–15; 1 John 3:12–15)

# RESISTING POPULAR OPINION

Then Caleb quieted the people before Moses, and said, "Let us go at once and take possession for we are well able to overcome it."
—Numbers 13:30

When assuming a new position, one of the first steps successful men almost always take is to get rid of everyone who spends more time talking about problems than about solutions. At times, standing for what is good and right means taking an unpopular position. In the biblical account of the Israelites' journey to the Promised Land, they sent spies to check it out before beginning their conquest. Two of the spies, Joshua and Caleb, came back and said, "No problem. We can take it." They were willing to do the unpopular thing and call the men to positive faith. Ten of the spies returned with frightening stories about how big the people were and how well their cities were fortified. This report was true, but they added that it would be impossible for them to conquer the land. The men listened to the ten who were fearful and spent forty years wandering in circles in the wilderness until that entire generation perished. Caleb saw the same giants and walled city as the other spies. He had surveyed the land, a reminder that faith is not blind. Faith does not deny the reality of difficulty; faith declares the power of God in the face of the problem. Kingdom warriors don't spend their lives going in circles, never fulfilling their potential and never reaching their Promised Land. Why? They listen more to the faithful than to those who are fearful. Faithful means "full of faith." If you are going to fulfill your destiny, you will need courage. Since Joshua and Caleb took that stand, they were the only ones of that generation who received what God had promised.

## Battle Plan

Ready yourself and claim what God has already promised! Stand your ground in faith. Surround yourself with courageous men (Psalm 60:12; Mark 9:23; Colossians 2:14–15).

# PERSEVERANCE IN ADVERSITY

For I know that my Redeemer lives, and He shall stand at last on the earth; and after my skin is destroyed this I know, that in my flesh I shall see God, Whom I shall see for myself and my eyes shall behold, and not another. How my heart yearns within me!
—Job 19:25–27

Great success usually comes at a great price. Nothing more than hope keeps a man going during adversity. We usually do everything that we can to avoid adversity. What comes cheaply usually has little value. Successful men in every field are those who refuse to be stopped. Job was a good man who suffered terribly without cause. The Bible says that he walked in complete integrity. Take time to read about his story. He fell into discouragement and asked God, "Why?" Job became so deeply depressed that at one time he wanted to stop breathing just to find some peace. Ever felt like that? You are not going to get where you are going without problems; no one does. Every bad thing that happens to you can either make you bitter or make you better. Bitter men never win. How did Job get through it? Even in the midst of his suffering, Job found encouragement in God's promise that he would one day meet his redeemer. "I have heard of You by the hearing of the ear, but now my eye sees You" (Job 42:5). Job's faith would become sight. That kind of perseverance can sustain a man even in the dark. Determine that you will get better and that every mountain you must climb is there to make you stronger. Men who stay resolutely on the course to fulfilling their goals, regardless of setbacks and disappointments, are the greatest warriors.

**Battle Plan**

Refuse to let obstacles stop you. Every opposing adversity is an opportunity to go higher with the right attitude (Psalm 17:15; Matthew 5:8; Romans 8:18–19; 1 John 3:2–3).

# THE PROBLEM WITH "POWER"

So it was, when Saul had turned his back to go
from Samuel, that God gave him another heart;
and all those signs came to pass that day.
—1 Samuel 10:9

The kingdom of God consists of transformed people. They think differently, they see differently, they hear differently, they act differently. In a word, we as men need to live differently. Why? Because we are different (kingdom warriors)! Saul, the man God chose as the first king of Israel, had a lot of "power" and was empowered by the Spirit of God. Sadly, he is a prime example of tremendous wasted potential. God had equipped Saul with everything he needed to succeed and had transformed this big, strong man to lead his people. However, Saul wasted his talents his gifts and his God-given opportunity to achieve greatness. Since Saul loved his power and position more than he loved God, he was often disobedient and offered lame excuses for his sin. As a result, he lost his power and position well before his time, leaving a sad legacy of failure as a king, father, and man of God. As men, in the kingdom, we need to understand that incomplete obedience is the same as disobedience (1 Samuel 15:22). What might Saul have accomplished if he had loved God wholeheartedly and kept His commandments? Although no one can say for sure, a look at the life of his successor, David, gives us some good clues. God has given us many talents and gifts so that we can be everything He wants us to be. God now invites us men who have an ear to hear and a heart to obey not only to reflect the kingdom's character but to experience the kingdom's ministry. Kingdom warriors! The question you and I must answer for us is this: What will I do with all that God has given me?

## Battle Plan

Obey completely. Don't substitute religion for obedience to God's Word (Mark 10:35–45; Romans 8:9–11; 2 Corinthians 5:17; Philippians 2:5–8).

# A FRESH APPROACH

That I may know Him and the power of His resurrection, and
the fellowship of His sufferings, being conformed to His death.
—Philippians 3:10

Any goal that is accomplished too quickly of too easily is probably
not a significant accomplishment. God is calling us to be kingdom
warriors! As we battle against the enemies of darkness, we need to
grasp the authority God has given us. That authority comes from
devoting oneself to knowing Jesus Christ. Paul's consuming passion,
having gained Christ, was to "be found in Him" as the source of his
life, as the branch to the Vine. Is this your consuming focus? Focus
itself is a great skill. Devotion focuses on the pursuit of intimacy
with God. Once we are focused, we must have the discipline to stay
focused. Any worthy goal will be more of a marathon than a sprint.
Paul had started in the runner's course; he was pressing on to grasp
actually for what Christ had already laid hold of him. The diversions
that distract us from the purposes of our lives can come from positive
or negative factors. Many men cannot see past the obstacles to attain
their goal, so they are tempted to seek easier goals. After you have

determined your goal, you must determine never to be diverted from it until you achieve it. We must become kingdom warriors! We know how our prayers affect heaven and earth. Most of us have been good students of spiritual warfare. But God is calling us to be more than a student of warfare. Your ultimate purpose is worthy of your attention every day. If you are not drawn to it daily in some way, it has probably not yet been set in your heart the way it must be if you are going to accomplish it.

**Battle Plan**

Make knowing Christ your main goal in life. Recite that goal in your heart every day. Write it on something that you can look at daily (Luke 9:23–26; 1 Corinthians 9:24–27; Hebrews 12:1–2).

# RISING TO THE GROUND

What have you here, and whom have you here, that you have
hewn a sepulcher here, as he who hews himself a sepulcher
on high, who carves a tomb for himself in a rock?
—Isaiah 22:16

Regardless of your specific circumstances, God has put you in a
place of leadership and authority so that you can selflessly and
humbly serve others. In a culture where ambition is praised as a
man's highest virtue, far too many Christian men adopt a "whatever
it takes" attitude toward rising up the ranks. Whether it's the business
associate who badmouths his peers to make himself look better to his
superiors or the pew-warmer (church spectator) who creates problems
in the congregation to further his own agenda, people take advantage
of opportunities for self-promotion that abound in this world. God
takes a dim view of such strategies. A kingdom warrior does not use
"worldly" strategies; he uses "kingdom" strategies. Worldly strategies
are cheap alternatives. A man named Shebna held a good deal of
power in the administration of King Hezekiah, but pride and vanity
ruled his heart. He used his high position to promote himself by

building a fancy tomb for his burial. In doing so, Shebna wrote his own ticket out of town. The Lord put a stop to his plans, removed him from office, and exiled him far from Judah (Isaiah 22:17–18). God gave Shebna everything he needed to become a great servant, but the foolish man squandered those good gifts by trying to rise to the top in his own selfish way. God wants to be at the center of *all* your plans. Your part in the equation as a kingdom warrior is to use all He has given you for His glory and the good of others. Remember, as Shebna did not, that God gives His gifts so that you may exalt Him, not yourself.

## Battle Plan

Humble yourself before God; trust Him to promote you as He wills. The higher the authority, the greater the accountability to God (Isaiah 22:15–19; 1 Corinthians 9:14–18; Philippians 3:17–19; 1 Peter 5:1–7).

# THE REAL DEAL

Demetrius has a good testimony from all, and from the truth itself. And we also bear witness, and you know that our testimony is true.

—3 John 1:12

Leaders in the kingdom are judged not so much by what they accomplish as by the character they reveal—who they are before what they do. There are significant qualities expected from leaders, which include spiritual preparedness, self-control, social graciousness, and holy living. Demetrius, a little-known believer briefly mentioned in John's third epistle, apparently had a good conduct. John tells us nothing about Demetrius except that people rightly spoke well of him. Can people say of you that your reputation, your conversation, and your behavior all demonstrate good character? Do your wife, children, and close friends see your character line up with the reputation at work or in public? The apostle contrasts Demetrius with a would-be leader named Diotrephes, whom he describes as a divisive man who made evil and false accusations against John. It is possible to have grand accomplishments and even religious behavior but still manifest a loveless, ungodly spirit. God loves to call men like

Demetrius to be a kingdom warrior because there is nothing phony about them, and people see them as the real deal. Though men like Diotrephes often attract a short-term following, sooner or later the truth comes out, and kingdom warriors like Demetrius lead a group to a healthier place. Are you the real deal?

**Battle Plan**

Nourish your true character and your reputation will take care of itself. Avoid those who are malicious gossips (Psalm 34:11–14; Romans 3:4; 1 Timothy 3:7; 1 John 2:28–29).

# GOING HALFWAY

Jehu took no heed to walk in the law of the Lord God
of Israel with all his heart; for he did not depart from
the sins of Jeroboam, who had made Israel sin.
—2 Kings 10:31

If you want to receive all the blessings God has for you, don't go halfway!
Kingdom warriors go all the way. God values our relationship with
Him more than He desires our service. Fathers want wholehearted
obedience from their sons. The same is true of our heavenly Father.
Jehu, a king of the northern kingdom of Israel, did some great things
for the Lord, but he was not fully devoted to the Lord. Jehu succeeded
as he followed God's specific instructions to remove the house of
Ahab and put an end to the worship of Baal in Israel. His work
earned commendations from God, and his descendants would have
positions of royalty for generations to come. However, because Jehu
served the Lord outwardly, God disciplined him with territorial
losses. Jehu's tolerance of other forms of idolatry cut short his reign
and brought about his personal destruction. Jehu learned that "going
halfway" is disobedience. What does wholehearted obedience to God

mean to you? God wants our hearts to be fully devoted to Him. The Lord is asking, "To what purpose is the multitude of your sacrifices to Me?" (Isaiah 1:11). Even zeal with an undevoted heart does not please Him. Empty-hearted sacrifice and soulless worship is not true devotion. Our hearts may not perceive or acknowledge that we are undevoted. At times, we may have no awareness of our spiritual state. Today, ask the Lord to enlighten your heart to any unacknowledged sin. He is waiting patiently for you right now.

**Battle Plan**

Be zealous for God with your whole heart. Dedicate your life to Him and to His purposes (Psalm 51:16–17; Proverbs 21:3; Ecclesiastes 5:1; Mark 12:33).

# HURRY UP AND WAIT

Therefore I will look to the Lord; I will wait for the
God of my salvation; my God will hear me.
—Micah 7:7

If you've served in the military, you have no doubt learned the meaning
of the expression "hurry up and wait." You wait in long lines to eat,
shower, shave, and use the restroom. Most men don't like to wait.
We want things to happen right now, but waiting always pays off. An
Old Testament prophet named Micah knew well the importance of
waiting confidently on God. His name means "who is like Yahweh."
He understood that regardless of how bad his circumstances might
be, the Lord would act on his behalf. Micah knew God's Word
always accomplishes the good for which it is intended. He didn't
just hope that God would act; rather, he expected God to move on
behalf of every man who remained faithful in prayer and carefully
followed through on what God had called him to do. The correct way
to hope and wait for the Lord is to steadfastly expect His mercy, His
salvation, and His rescue and, while waiting, not take matters into
your own hands. Are you waiting for God to do His part without

running ahead of Him? Receiving God's best in every area of your life often means waiting for Him to do what He has promised. How will you respond if He keeps you in suspense?

## Battle Plan

Hurry up and wait on God. You will reap in due season if you faint not. Wait! (Psalm 130; Isaiah 40:29–31; Lamentations 3:22–27; Romans 8:24–25; 2 Corinthians 4:8–18)

# REVENGE IS EXPENSIVE

Now when Abner had returned to Hebron, Joab took him aside
in the gate to speak with him privately, and there stabbed him in
the stomach, so that he died for the blood of Asahel his brother.
—2 Samuel 3:27

Every act of vengeance you ponder and every plan you make for
getting even costs you part of who God made you to be. When
someone does you wrong, even intentionally, make it your business
to forgive that person and to move on so that you can continue to
pursue the good things that God has placed before you. Revenge
can cost both parties dearly. As an example, look at the life of Joab,
the nephew and army commander of King David. Joab had served
the king faithfully and had enjoyed success in his military career,
rising to the office of top general. He failed because he used his
high position to settle old scores- namely, the death of his brother
Asahel at the hand of Abner, the uncle of Saul, the former king of
Israel (2 Samuel 2:18–32). At an opportune time, Joab lured Abner,
once an enemy of David but now ready to make peace, to the gate of
Hebron and murdered him, thus avenging his brother's death while

eliminating a potential rival. Joab had his revenge, but it came at a steep price. When word reached David about what had happened, the king praised Abner but cursed Joab and his family (2 Samuel 3:28–29). Although Joab continued to serve David, when he indulged in vengeance instead of using his position appropriately, he lost an important part of himself. He also planted the seeds of his own destruction which cost him his life (1 Kings 2:5–6; 28–35). What a price!

**Battle Plan**

Renounce any form of retaliation. Leave all vengeance to God (2 Samuel 3:22–39; Proverbs 25:21–22; Matthew 5:38–42; Romans 12:9–21).

# SECOND CHANCES

But Naaman became furious and went away and said, "Indeed,
I said to myself, He will surely come out to me, and stand
and wave his hand over the place, and heal the leprosy."
—2 Kings 5:11

No man stays at the pinnacle of success forever, and most do not stay there very long. Naaman the Syrian general was a good man and even the meaning of his name is defined as "pleasant." His leprosy was not the result of his wrongdoing. All of these great military exploits said about Naaman did not save or heal him; he was still a leper. And so are the many men in the world who think their state, status, and position mean something with God. They don't! However, when our slide begins, it is seldom wise to strive to stay at the top. Remember the lessons we learned that enabled us to get there, and then look for another path to use them again. When the prophet Elisha heard of his condition, he sent for Naaman, but when Naaman arrived at Elisha's home, he was disappointed and angered when the prophet just sent instructions to dip seven times in the Jordon River. Naaman expects to be waited on attention; but Elisha just tells him what to do. His human brashness and hidden pride were surfaced, and his obedience and submission opened the way to healing. When he obeyed, his leprosy disappeared. Naaman found out that day the God of Israel is a God of second chances. This warrior found healing. More importantly, he found salvation in the kingdom of God. Listen to this "kingdom warrior" as his shouts his allegiance to his "new *King*": "I know now that there is no God in all the world except in Israel" (2 Kings 5:15–18).

## Battle Plan

Salvation makes a man "whole." Above all follow and obey the Lord. Allow the Lord to replace old deceptions with a new belief system that will bring us to success (Mark 16:15–18; 1 Corinthians 1:17–18; Galatians 6:14)!

# SHADY CHARACTER

*Reuben, you are my firstborn, my might and the beginning
of my strength, the excellency of dignity and the excellency
of power. Unstable as water, you shall not excel.*

—Genesis 49:3–4

People look to you—as a man of God, a husband, and a father—for
stability. A kingdom warrior lifestyle requires radical change in your
life. A worldly character can become a source of destruction to you
and those around you when things get out of control. Reuben, the
firstborn son of Jacob, did some very good things in life. For example,
he spoke up on behalf of his brother Joseph and saved his life when
the other brothers wanted to kill him (Genesis 37:21–22). Reuben
pledged his own sons' lives when Jacob refused to allow Benjamin to
travel to Egypt with him (Genesis 42:37). Reuben forfeited the place
of fame and special promises because he committed a horrible sin.
He slept with one of his father's concubines; an act that Jacob never
forgot (Genesis 35:22). As his father said, "Reuben you are unstable
and you shall not excel" (Genesis 49:4). Reuben illustrates a life of
unfulfilled potential and missed opportunity. No one can say what

would have happened to Reuben's family had he conducted himself as a godly man and not become shady—"unstable as water." Would you call yourself a godly man? Or are you out of control "unstable as water"? King Solomon warns, a man out of control with no limits is no man (Proverbs 25:28). Allow your character to be under God's control today. Remember, that an effective and productive life results in "character transformation." Sounds simple doesn't it? But it is far from easy. Go through your day in God's strength not yours.

**Battle Plan**

Honor commitments and your word even when it is costly to do so. Don't conduct your life as the world does! (Psalm 15; Galatians 5:22–23; 2 Peter 1:5–11)

# KINGDOM FATHERHOOD

O my Lord, please let the Man of God whom You sent come to us
again and teach us what we shall do for the child who will be born.
—Judges 13:8

Fathers hold a most unique and challenging role in God's order—we
are responsible to raise the next generation of the kingdom of God.
God entrusts children to fathers, allowing His own nurturing heart
to flow through them to the children. Part of having a heart like the
Lord's heart requires that we recognize the fact that loving and caring
for children honors God. Manoah, the father of the Israelite judge
Samson, gives us a good example of a man (kingdom warrior) who
was humble and smart enough to ask for some divine confirmation.
Manoah was a kingdom warrior for his marriage and family! An
angel had appeared to his childless wife, informing her that she
would give birth to a very special son who should be dedicated to the
Lord's service. The angel also laid out the ground rules for raising
the boy. No doubt, Manoah felt apprehensive about the birth of his
son. He desired to know more. Wouldn't you as a husband? Instead
of just wondering and worrying, he did what any kingdom warrior in

need of confirmation should do: he asked God for help. Our prayers are mighty under God, to invite His kingdom into our affairs. God answered Manoah's prayer of faith. The angel soon returned to give him the confirmation he needed to take on the task of fathering such a special little boy. Does anything in your marriage, family, or work life make you wonder which way to turn? Ask God for help. Do you require a little confirmation for some plan you have in mind? Stop right now and ask the Lord to show you. Prayer invites God's rule.

## Battle Plan

Get down to the nitty-gritty of practical fatherhood. Seek the Lord and ask for what you need (Psalm 78:5–8; Psalm 127; Proverbs 22:6; 2 Timothy 3:14–15; James 1:5).

# MIGHTY MAN OF VALOR

And the Angel of the Lord appeared to him, and said to
him, "The Lord is with you, you mighty man of valor"!
—Judges 6:12

At times in your life of faith when you're not sure what God has
called you to do, it's not a bad idea to ask for confirmation. God has
wired each man differently as kingdom warriors. Some move out
courageously and say, "Let's get started!" while others need to test
the waters before taking their steps of faith. Gideon was a man of
God who needed to be sure. God sent word to Gideon of His desire
through an angel. The message was simple, "The Lord is with you."
God called Gideon by the meaning of his name "might warrior,"
even though in his own eyes he was just as any other man. The entire
theme of Gideon's life has to do with God proving Himself over
and over again to a man that needed constant affirmation. We often
question God when we don't understand the hardships that impact
our lives. Our own abilities, endurance, and power will run out in
the midst of overwhelming hardships. But when the Lord is with us,
He will sustain us right in the middle of our deadening blows. We

all need that reassurance at times, don't we? When Gideon asked God for many signs, confirmations, and proof, he wanted to know without a doubt that he understood God's calling. He simply needed help believing in what God had said. God wasn't angry when Gideon asked Him to confirm His commands, and He won't be angry with you, either. Praise the Lord! God gave Israel and Gideon a miracle that surpassed and battle strategy. The Lord brought deliverance through a man that needed continual reassurance. The fact remains (Judges 8)! The Lord is faithful even when we need Him to prove it to us "one more time." Rise up and take your position, for today you are that mighty man of valor!

**Battle Plan**

Believe that God strengthens those He calls and commissions (Joel 3:9–10; Zechariah 4:6; Psalm 83; 1 Corinthians 1:26–31).

# NO WEAPONS, JUST SHOUTS

Now Joshua had commanded the people, saying, "You
shall not shout or make any noise with your voice,
nor shall a word proceed out of your mouth, until the
day I say to you, "shout"! then you shall shout."
—Joshua 6:10

The ability to lead others through the changes without hurting their morale is usually what separates good kingdom warriors from great ones. In Joshua 6, God revealed His battle plan to Joshua. "Joshua, pay attention," God said. "Go around the walls for six days. On the seventh day, go seven times around the wall. Nobody says a word. After the seventh time, sever priests blow seven trumpets, and everyone shouts. That's the plan." This plan resembled nothing that Joshua had ever heard of or experienced. Have you ever gone to God in a time of crisis and He answered with something that seemed so ridiculous? The Israelites had no weapons, no battering rams, and no means by which they might overcome the city of Jericho. Can you imagine how this band of former slaves appeared to their enemy? No doubt, they were tempted to speak words of doubt as they went around day after day. They may have been tempted to criticize their leader, not understanding the purpose of what they were doing. But they nonetheless obeyed. The true measure of a true kingdom warrior is whether he obeys. The Wall of Jericho, that mighty fortress in which their enemies trusted, fell down. It was completely removed as though it never existed. What walls stand between you and your promise? Is it sickness, despair, financial trouble, or a family member broken your heart? No wall is too big for God! Just close your mouth and march. Get ready to shout! The walls that have been holding you back are about to fall!

## Battle Plan

Be still as God works. You will see His deliverance (Exodus 14:13–14; Psalm 18:29–34, all of 46; Romans 10:11–13).

# IS THERE NOT A CAUSE?

Then David said to the Philistine, "You come to me
with a sword, with a spear, and with a javelin. But I
come to you in the name of the Lord of hosts, the God
of the armies of Israel, whom you have defied."
—1 Samuel 17:45

Have you ever felt inadequate for the task to which God was calling
you? Have you ever stood alone on the battlefield with an adversary
who outmatched you in every area of warfare? This was the situation
Israel faced from the Philistine army in 1 Samuel 17. The Bible paints
a terrifying picture of the giant Goliath. This killing machine was
huge, strong, and highly skilled as a warrior. No one in Saul's army
had the nerve to confront him. God will use anyone and anything
to bring deliverance, and it will not always come in a form that we
recognize or desire. The man that was most likely to meet Goliath
on the battlefield was Saul. After all, he was the king. As far as we
know, Saul never got out of his tent, but he was more than willing
to send David where he was not willing to go himself. Still, to most
observers, this spirited shepherd boy was a decided underdog. David

didn't see himself that way at all. David knew that God had sent him on this mission, and God never sends a man to fight without equipping and guiding him to accomplish His purposes. Goliath had nothing but a slingshot and five smooth stones. There was another weapon David held that was more important to him that day. This weapon was held not in his hands but in his heart. David had an unshakable faith in God, who was bigger than any giant. David was literally the instrument used to gain a great victory over God's enemies. What "giants" in your life, at home, at work, or other areas make you feel like the underdog? There is a cause! God wants to use you, and He is waiting to see who will be His champions! Why shouldn't it be you?

**Battle Plan**

Don't fear opposition even when it seems stronger or better supported. God can use your minimal resources (Exodus 15:3; Psalm 24:8; Romans 8:37; 2 Corinthians 10:4).

# NO WEAPONS, JUST PRAISE

And when Jehoshaphat had consulted with the people, he
appointed those who should sing to the Lord, and who should
praise the beauty of holiness, as they went out before the army and
were saying: "Praise the Lord, For His mercy endures forever."
—2 Chronicles 20:21

God gives us strategies that are not the wisdom of this world. In 2
Chronicles 20, God gives us a great lesson on the power of praise. The
example God has presented to us is to send Judah first, not necessarily
the wisest or the strongest. The name Judah means "praise." As men,
we need to allow praise to lead the way. Unshakable praise breaks
through! It is this kind of praise that God sends first, not praise that
is dependent on the circumstances, because the circumstances might
not always be favorable. Judah was confronted by mortal enemies,
Moab and Ammon. The people sought God in prayer and with
faith in His Word. Then came the word of the prophet: "Do not be
afraid … for the battle is not yours, but God's (v. 15). The victory
came in a strange but powerful manner. As the army of God praised
the Lord with a loud voice, God sent confusion into the enemy's camp,

causing them to fall upon and slay one another. Praise in the midst of the battle will always cause the enemy's plans to be thrown into turmoil. Jehoshaphat was able to win the day by sending his praise team first (2 Chronicles 20:20–22). One of the greatest mysteries is that we become something beyond what we are as individuals when we, as kingdom warriors, assemble. What would happen if we came together in a place of praise and worship (having church), where we all responded fully to the Lord as kingdom warriors?

**Battle Plan**

Believe in praise as a mighty, effectual spiritual weapon (Exodus 17:11–12; Psalm 150; Acts 16:25–26; Ephesians 5:18–19).

# IT AIN'T OVER 'TIL
# GOD SAYS SO!

Now behold, an angel of the Lord stood by him, and a light shone
in the prison; and he struck Peter on the side and raised him
up, saying, "Arise quickly!" And his chains fell off his hands.
—Acts 12:7

Are you facing what seems like an impossible situation, whether at
home, at work, in your marriage, or somewhere else? If so, remember
that it's not over until God says it's over. He will never abandon you,
but He will enable you to complete whatever He has planned for you.
The apostle Peter could say a hearty amen to that statement. The
time came when it seemed that his life had come to an end. Herod
wanted Peter dead and had already murdered other believers. As
Peter sat in a jail cell awaiting a rigged trial, he must have wondered
how many hours he had left. God had another strategy. On the night
before Peter's trial, an angel appeared in his prison cell, awakened
him, released him from his chains, and led him past the guards to
freedom. At first, even Peter couldn't fully grasp what had happened.
As he came out of his stupor, he realized that his "dream" was

real—God had set him free! Peter's experience shows that none of the enemy's chains are strong enough to hold down a man of God whom has been called to complete a specific purpose and mission. What's your situation in this hour? Can you recognize the hand of God at work? Neither God nor the angel did what Peter could only do for himself. Peter had to put on his garments and sandals and follow. Likewise, nothing can hinder our escape from the enemy as we rise to obey the Lord. After this, the Word of God grew and multiplied. Our ultimate deliverance is drawing nigh!

## Battle Plan

Give corporate prayer a central place in your life. This will reverse the enemy's plan and bring restoration into the lives of those you pray for (Deuteronomy 32:30–31; Psalm 34; Matthew 6:9–13; Acts 12:1–17).

# NO WEAPONS, JUST PRAYER

Now therefore, O Lord our God, save us from
his hand, that all the kingdoms of the earth may
know that You are the Lord, You alone.
—Isaiah 37:20

It is not our job to go about making our own judgments in any situation. God is not obligated to answer prayers that are spoken without having entered into counsel with Him first. We are to move in response to Him, not the other way around. In Isaiah 37, Jerusalem was under siege, and the nation was facing death-dealing adversity. The Assyrian army was the worlds dominate power, and they were coming against Jerusalem making bold threats. The Jewish nation had diminished in size and strength by more than 80 percent, both in their military force and their territory. Judah's king, Hezekiah, knew there was no way that Jerusalem could stand up against this army. When we face situations feeling as though we have reached our limit, our strength is to call on the Lord! In the face of our weakness, the Lord's strength is made perfect in weakness! Hezekiah does not react to the threats of his enemy but cries out to the Lord for help.

It was then that the prophet Isaiah sent Hezekiah a prophetic word. Strength for victory would not be based on human energy, but on the will to pray. The Assyrian's defeat was the result of earnest prayer by Hezekiah. Our prayers are effective when, as men, we are seeking God's intentions. Ask God to help you to discern your situation so that you can move in prayer power. The deliverance prophesied by Isaiah came in the form of a death angel that killed 185,000 Assyrians (Isaiah 37:36–38). There is power in prayer! No weapon used just calling on the Lord.

**Battle Plan**

Seek the Lord today. Wait on Him to speak to your heart and spirit (Psalm 5:1–3; Acts 4:31–34; Romans 8:26; James 5:13–18).

# FROM RAGS TO ROYALTY

So David said to him, "Do not fear, for I will surely
show you kindness for Jonathan your father's sake, and
will restore to you all the land of Saul your grandfather;
and you shall eat bread at my table continually."
—2 Samuel 9:7

Once you realize the scandalous depths of God's love, change
becomes possible. God will never give up on you despite how many
times you've given up on yourself. God's grace will give you the
courage to look at your woundedness, but then you have to move
beyond it. As an example, look at the life of Mephiboseth, who was
five years old when Saul and Jonathan were killed. When the news
about their death came from the city of Jezreel, his nurse picked him
up and fled; but she was in such a hurry that she dropped him and
he became "lame in his feet," he was crippled (2 Sam. 4:4). You have
probably never been crippled physically, but all of us as men have
been crippled within by our own sins and mistakes of others. Most
guys have been dropped by somebody along the way. Most likely
this was someone they were counting on, someone who should have

been supportive or responsible. This trauma has its effects in the way you deal with others and hampers your ability to relate and trust. No, we don't blame other people for our struggles! Why? Kingdom warriors don't blame; we reclaim! King David sought out this son of Jonathan in order to bless him. Mephibosheth had to decide to come to the king's table. This meant he had to get up off the floor of shame. That's exactly what he did (2 Samuel 9:13). Mephibosheth sat at the table of blessing as if nothing tough had ever happened to him. No, he wasn't pretending or denying his brokenness. He was letting the *King* cover and bless him. Despite his limitations, Mephibosheth came to know he belonged at the table of "Grace." You'll do the same.

## Battle Plan

Pray constantly for your inner man to be strengthened so you might live a life that honors God. Come to God without any masks or hidden areas; He will carry you (2 Samuel 9:1–13; Ephesians 3:14–19; Colossians 1:9–14).

# HUMBLE-MINDED COURAGE

Serving the Lord with all humility, with many tears and
trials which happened to me by the plotting of the Jews; and
how I kept back nothing that was helpful, but proclaimed it
to you, and taught you publicly and from house to house.
—Acts 20:19–20

What image comes to mind when you think of courage? Perhaps we imagine movies like *Rambo* or *Gladiator*, where the warrior is not influenced by pain and injury. When most men think of courage, they don't also think of humility. As men of God, we know that we are to serve Him with humility. We also know that we fight in a spiritual battle. But a close look at the Bible reveals much about God's plan for courage that flows from humility. The apostle Paul had both qualities. He never seemed to concern himself with the consequences of his unpopular preaching. He knew that lifting up the name of Jesus Christ meant trouble and persecution, but he preached anyway. His courage flowed from his conviction that God wanted him to share the truth of forgiveness and restoration from God through Jesus Christ. Simply put, godliness is living the way God wants us to—as kingdom warriors! Wimps don't trust, rely on, or obey God. That requires courage and humility, which wimps lack. Understand that your conduct is the most effective sermon you will ever preach. You have probably never met anyone as courageous as Paul, but he would be the first to tell you that his courage was dependent on his humble reliance on God's strength, not on his own abilities. When you have a humble attitude of unselfish concern for the welfare of others—no one will mistake you for a wimp. Instead, a kingdom man with courage—a kingdom warrior.

**Battle Plan**

Live a life that will give consistent, undeniable evidence of the truth of the gospel (Matthew 11:28–30; Ephesians 4:1–3; Colossians 3:12–14; 1 Peter 5:5–7).

# ENDURING FAITHFULNESS

And Uriah said to David, "The ark and Israel and Judah
are dwelling in tents, and my lord Joab and the servants of
my lord are encamped in the open fields. Shall I then go
to my house to eat and drink, and to live with my wife? as
you live, and as your soul lives, I will not do this thing."
—2 Samuel 11:11

God never promises that faithfulness and loyalty will be rewarded
or even recognized in this life. An Old Testament warrior named
Uriah the Hittite, one of King David's mighty men, provides an
example. Uriah had no way of knowing that his master, King David,
had already wronged him by seducing and impregnating his wife.
David's invitation for Uriah to stay home, take it easy, and spend the
night with Bathsheba was just an attempt to cover David's own sin.
It is admirable when a friend remains loyal and faithful even when
treated shamefully. Uriah knew that he couldn't in good conscience
stay home with his wife while his men were fighting during the day
and sleeping in tents at night. Uriah's loyalty to David and his men
cost him dearly because the guilt-ridden David hatched another plan

to cover his sin and had Uriah killed in battle. Uriah did his duty and demonstrated the godly traits of faithfulness and loyalty. The people in your life need you to remain faithful and loyal to them, to God, and to His Word. God will reward those who honor Him. Uriah encourages us to think beyond human history. His life honored King David and the men he fought alongside. His faithfulness and loyalty cost him his life on earth, but he continues to encourage us from his honored place in heaven to make faithfulness and loyalty high priorities. "Be faithful until death, and I [Jesus] will give you the crown of life" (Revelation 2:10).

## Battle Plan

Be faithful to Jesus when confronted with death. Faith's commitment to overcome does not fear even death (2 Samuel 11; Psalm 31:23–24; Proverbs 20:6; Matthew 25:23).

# HEARING GOD BY REVELATION

Jesus said to them, "But who do you say that I am?" Simon Peter answered and said, "You are the Christ, the Son of the living God."
—Matthew 16:15–16

At Caesarea Philippi, a stronghold of the ancient demon-gods of Syria, Greece, and Rome, Jesus deliberately set Himself against the background of the world's religions' error and confusion; and here He inquired of His disciples about His identity. Peter didn't need to hear the opinions of others to know who Jesus was because God had already shown him. The godly man "hears" God; that is, his spirit is tuned to the promptings of the Holy Spirit. The disciples had heard rumors about their Master, and they weren't afraid to tell Him. Some thought He was John the Baptist resurrected, while others thought He was Elijah of another prophet returned to earth. But one day, Jesus asked them the question that would shape their lives for all eternity: "Who do you say I am?" There was probably a moment of silence as the disciples wracked their brains to figure out how to answer Jesus. It's not surprising that Peter, the one willing to say what the others only thought, finally spoke up. Out of his mouth came the most blessed answer far beyond human reason: "You are the Christ, the Son of the living God." Peter, a simple fisherman with no formal training, education, or theology, knew that Jesus was that Man—and much, much more. Jesus answered and said to him, "Blessed are you, Simon Bar-Jonah, for flesh and blood has not revealed this to you, but my Father who is in heaven" (Matthew 16:17). How you answer the question of who Jesus is will shape your entire being. Peter correctly answered! Will you? Who do you say Jesus is?

**Battle Plan**

Pray to know Christ more and to understand God's purpose and power in your life by His Word (Matthew 16:13–20; Acts 26:15–18; Ephesians 1:17–18; 3:14–19; Colossians 1:9–12).

# BLESS YOUR WIFE

O my love, you are as beautiful as Tirzah, lovely as
Jerusalem, awesome as an army with banners!
—Song of Solomon 6:4

Many wives complain that their husbands take them for granted.
They worry that the excitement has gone from their marriage and
that the passion and fun have faded away. Your wife is "royalty." She
is a daughter of the King. As kingdom warriors, we need to take
time to compliment our wives and affirm their inward and outward
beauty. Make sure that you speak those words out of genuine desire
to affirm her and build her up. Solomon understood the value of
speaking passionately to his beloved Shulamite woman. He knew
that in expressing his deepest feelings for her, he could bless her
and stir up passion between them. Precious words of endearment
flew back and forth between Solomon and his beloved. The words
that Solomon and his lover spoke to one another model the kind of
intimate communication you can enjoy with your wife. Of course, it's
a good idea to speak your own words as you express how much your
wife means to you. Such words are personal and thoughtful. How

do you rate the passion and fun in your marriage? Would you say that it's red hot, still glowing, like a fading ember, or growing cold? To help bring back the flame, regularly speak words of appreciation and love to the wife God has given you. Take the lead, husband! Ponder what you find most valuable, beautiful, and sexy about your wife, and then make a point of telling her how much you like what you see. You won't regret it! The romance in your marriage will be refreshed and renewed.

## Battle Plan

Speak words of love that caress your wife's soul. Study the lost art of verbal lovemaking (Song of Solomon 6:4–10; Ephesians 5:25–29; Colossians 3:19).

# LOOK PAST YOUR
# SHORTCOMINGS

Moses said to God, "Who am I that I should go to
Pharaoh, and bring the children of Israel out of Egypt?"
So God said, "I will certainly be with you."
—Exodus 3:11–12

Think of the last time that you felt way over your head. Maybe it was a conflict with your wife that just could not work out. Perhaps you couldn't understand your child's rebellious behavior. In life, as our role of being husbands and fathers, it has a way of overwhelming us at times. The good news for every kingdom warrior is that when you feel inadequate, God has you right where He wants you. Moses felt ill-equipped when he heard God's command to return to Egypt. Surely, Moses felt like we all feel when an overwhelming problem or challenge confronts us. Do you have a problem at work that you can't get past? Did a falling out with a friend cause relational damage that you don't know how to fix? A man is in a great place when he has no one to turn to but God. With only God to help, we are in an excellent place; that is where God works a miracle. Moses focused on himself when he needed to focus on God. Certainly, you have weaknesses; we all do. God didn't remove Moses's weaknesses when He called him into leadership, but God did promise Moses His presence, and God makes this same promise to you. Hear God speak to you and say, "I Am Who I Am, I Am has sent you" (Exodus 3:14). Do you think God will do any less for you than He did for Moses? God waits for us to act! Arise, you mighty kingdom warrior!

## Battle Plan

Understand that God's Name is "I Am Who I Am!" Rest on this foundation. Be grounded and established in Him (Psalm 86; Isaiah 30:21; John 1:11–12).

# SPIRITUAL DISCERNMENT

Of the children of Issachar who had understanding of the
times, to know what Israel ought to do, their chiefs were two
hundred; and all their brethren were at their command.
—1 Chronicles 12:32

Whom do you picture as a person who understands our times? You
probably think of a man in political or military leadership who knows
how to deal with the forces currently affecting us. The Bible tells us
that the men of Issachar not only understood the times in which they
lived but also knew what should be done. That is a rare and valuable
gift. These kingdom warriors fought for king David and helped him
form effective strategies for defending Israel from all treats. They
were the brains of David's military and used their God-given wisdom
to discern what was best for the kingdom. The men of Issachar had
the all-important trait of discernment that we all need. Like Israel
during David's reign, we live in perilous times. You don't have to be
a political or military leader to be a man of discernment. As a man
of God, a husband, a father, a boss, or an employee, you have the
opportunity to make an impact. As kingdom warriors, we will not

lead successfully unless we know where we are going. We will not discern the present or see the future with perfect accuracy. If the Spirit of Christ dwells within you (as He lives in the heart of every genuine believer), you have all the resources you need to be a man of discernment. God calls us, as kingdom warriors, to understand our own times, and He will give us the wisdom and insight to know what to do, what to say, and what to pray. The world has never needed you more.

## Battle Plan

Daily ask God for discernment. Be assured that victory is already yours in Christ (Psalm 119:17–24; 1 Corinthians 2:6–16; 1 John 4:1–6).

# GOD'S PURPOSE FOR GOOD

Judah said to his brothers, "What profit is there if we kill our
brother and conceal his blood?" "Come and let us sell him
to the Ishmaelites, and let not our hand be upon him, for he
is our brother and our flesh." and his brothers listened.
—Genesis 37:26–27

There's something courageous about a character that sees survival
as a blessing, especially in the face of undeserved abuse. Even in
hardship, suffering, bitter disappointments, even when wrongly
treated, kingdom warriors can know that God will work in such
situations to fulfill His "good purpose." God doesn't guarantee you
problem-free days on earth. Just ask Joseph, who endured more than
his share of unfair abuse. Joseph didn't suffer at the hands of strangers
but as the victim of his jealous brothers. Their father, Jacob, expressed
favoritism toward Joseph; as a result, the brothers nurtured a hatred
for their younger sibling. When they caught him walking alone in the
desert one day, they sold him to a band of traders and told his father
that a wild animal had killed him. Joseph determined to live for God
regardless of his circumstances. He understood the adversity was a

fire by which God was seeking to purify his life. That courageous choice to deny bitterness and to pray allowed Joseph to be able to perceive the hand of God in his suffering. Joseph said to his brothers, "You meant evil against me; but God meant it for good, in order to bring it about as it is this day, to save many people alive" (Genesis 50:20). God will use your circumstances for your good and the good of God's people. Allow Him to work in you and through your life today. A blessing is just around the corner.

## Battle Plan

Trust God to cause all things to work for your good as you remain faithful to His calling and purpose (Psalm 66:8–12; Romans 8:18–30; Job 13:15–16; Malachi 3:2–3).

# ARE YOU STEADFAST?

Now when Daniel knew that the writing [law] was
signed, he went home. And in his upper room, with his
windows open toward Jerusalem, he knelt down on his
knees three times that day, and prayed and gave thanks
before his God, as was his custom since early days.
—Daniel 6:10

The right combination of vision and values is the most powerful
force for change the world can ever know. Many have vision but no
values. Others have values but no vision. Our goal is to be steadfast,
in both vision and values. God calls you to be a steadfast man who
refuses to compromise the well-being of your family or the dignity
of your work or ministry even when you face hard choices. The
Old Testament prophet Daniel knew the importance of remaining
steadfast in difficult times. His enemies had duped king Darius into
creating a law that outlawed all forms of worship except worship of
the king. The penalty for breaking the law was death at the jaws of
hungry lions. Daniel was faced with a terrible choice: either worship
Darius and live or continue faithfully praying to God and be cast into

the den of lions. Daniel loved God, so he refused to bow in worship before a man. In fact, when he heard of the new law, he headed to his room and prayed fervently. His enemies observed his defiance and had him thrown into the lions' den. What temptations are whispered in your ears that would compromise your faithfulness to God? Like Daniel, God will honor our steadfast faithfulness and deliver us from the enemy's pit. "My God sent His angel and shut the lions' mouths, so that they have not hurt me" (Daniel 6:22). Daniel didn't receive so much as a scratch.

## Battle Plan

Never give up! Remain steadfast in your commitment to God, no matter what (Psalm 1; Romans 12:9–21; 1 Corinthians 10:13, 15:58).

# USE THE SECULAR
# FOR HIS GLORY

And Bezalel and Aholiab, and every gifted artisan in whom
the Lord has put wisdom and understanding, to know how
to do all manner of work for the service of the sanctuary,
shall do according to all that the Lord has commanded.
—Exodus 36:1

Do you have a hard time believing that God can make powerful
use of a regular working man, such as a bus driver, custodian, clerk,
or concrete worker? Do you believe that God only uses the "pros"
to do ministry? If so, it may be time to expand your thinking. Too
often, we make unnecessary distinctions between the holy and the
secular skills. God wants us to understand that He has given us all
our gifts and talents, even those that don't seem spiritual in nature.
As kingdom warriors, God wants us to use whatever gifts we have
for His glory. God had a specific job in mind for two artisans named
Bezalel and Aholiab. When the time came to build a Tabernacle in
the wilderness, God called them to use their gifts and skills for "His
Glory." When these two craftsmen left Egypt with their countrymen

as part of the exodus, did they have any idea that God would use their abilities in amazing ways? How could they? Bezalel and Aholiab had no idea what a tabernacle was, let alone how their skills could be used to build one. But God had given this pair their skills, and when He asked them to put their abilities into action, they willingly made them available. It's not just your capability but God wants your availability in His kingdom. A kingdom warrior shows up ready for service! Listen, God loves to use unexpected resources for purposes we could never have imagined. Our role, as kingdom warriors in the kingdom of God, is to do as Bezalel and Aholiab did—make whatever secular talents we have available for the Lord's use. Why? God gave them to us in the first place!

**Battle Plan**

Put your skills in God's hands. Then watch God do amazing things for the benefit of His people (Exodus 35:30–36:7; 1 Corinthians 12:12–31; Revelation 3:7–13).

# WHAT'S ON YOUR TO-DO LIST?

Then Jeshua the son of Jozadak and his brethren the priests,
and Zerubbabel the son of Shealtiel and his brethren, arose
and built the altar of the God of Israel, to offer burnt offerings
on it, as it is written in the Law of Moses the man of God.

—Ezra 3:2

Sometimes, it's good to stop and ask yourself what tops your "to-do list." So, what is it? You have lists of things to do at home before you go to work and lists of things to do at work before you can go home. Don't forget, come the weekend, there are more lists. And the cycle goes on and on. You know those things that prevent us from spending time with God, chores to do, kids to spend time with, ball games to attend, calls to be returned. Then, of course, there's your wife, who needs at least some of your undivided attention. Jeshua and Zerubbabel were called to lead their people back to Jerusalem following the Babylonian captivity. These two, kingdom warriors, created extra work when they insisted on making provisions for worship before rebuilding the city's walls. Can you imagine the worry setting in as the people looked at the devastated city? One can only wonder the questions they asked. Can't building the altar wait? Don't you understand the danger we face? We'll have plenty of time to worship after we get the wall built. Our enemies want to kill us! Listen, these are legitimate concerns, but these two kingdom warriors knew what they were doing. They understood that unless they placed the worship of God at the top of their "to-do list," nothing else would matter. Also, they remembered that the people who built the original walls had forgotten to put God at the top of their list. As result, their walls came tumbling down. A kingdom warrior makes time with God his top priority. When we do this, we invite God to bless all the other things on "our list."

## Battle Plan

Be faithful to God, and beware of what hinders you from spending time with God (Psalm 63; Jeremiah 29:13; Matthew 6:33–34; Luke 12:31–34; James 4:13–17).

# MOVE AND LEAVE THE
# PAST BEHIND

Now Barnabas was determined to take with them John
called Mark. But Paul insisted that they should not
take with them the one who had departed from them in
Pamphylia, and had not gone with them to the work.
—Acts 15:37–38

Do you believe that past failures disqualify you from effective service
in God's kingdom? Everyone fails at one time or another. Kingdom
warriors see failure as an opportunity for growth! If you do you might
be encouraged to keep trying and keep going. What's the result?
We bury our past failures in Jesus. Without question, our Christian
life thrives on this principle. A young kingdom warrior named John
Mark (the Mark who wrote the Second Gospel) shows us how it
works. John Mark had accompanied Paul and Barnabas on their first
missionary journey, only to leave the team, possibly because he was
homesick and frightened (Acts 13:13). Later, as Paul and Barnabas
were preparing for another missionary journey, Barnabas wanted to
give John Mark another chance. Paul disagreed, and the two parted

ways (Acts 15:36–40). Barnabas saw something worth developing in John Mark's life and started mentoring him. Paul later changed his mind about the young warrior (Colossians 4:10) and eventually recognized him as an effective minister who had the right stuff after all (2 Timothy 4:11). Some of the greatest ministers of all time failed early on but later grew to be solid men of God. What does it take to be a solid kingdom warrior? It takes courage to keep going—to "move and leave the past behind."

## Battle Plan

Aim to achieve what God has and leave past failures behind! Spare no cost! Spare no effort! (1 Corinthians 9:24–27; Philippians 3:12–16; 2 Timothy 4:7)

# SEEING THE BIGGER PICTURE

*For the vision is yet for an appointed time; but at the end
it will speak, and it will not lie. Though it tarries, wait
for it; because it will surely come, it will not tarry.*
—Habakkuk 2:3

Getting a specific vision is crucial if we are going to succeed. There are circumstances that may dictate a course change. Men, we must view every day of our lives as a school that is meant to prepare us for where we are heading. What we think about and focus on affects our attitude, especially when things go wrong. The prophet Habakkuk lamented the spiritual condition of his people and the consequences of the coming destruction of Jerusalem and the Babylonian captivity that would follow. Habakkuk grieved over this situation, but he didn't sink into despair or allow his circumstances to rob him of his joy in serving and loving God. He saw the bigger picture! To him, joy in God was a choice, Babylonians or no Babylonians. "Yet I will rejoice in the Lord!" he cried. "I will be joyful in the God of my salvation!" (Habakkuk 3:18). Men who leave their mark on the world do not just arrive at their destination; they make the way for everyone else to get there easier. Habakkuk focused on the positive, not the deplorable situation around him. He recorded biblical promises God made alive to him. The Lord told him, "Write the vision and make it plain on tablets, that he may he may run who reads it" (Habakkuk 2:2). Listen as the Lord speaks to you, mighty warrior!

## Battle Plan

Look with the eyes of faith at God's plan for the future. Rest in and rely on God's constant love and provision (Psalm 74:9–17; Proverbs 29:18; James 5:7–8; 2 Peter 3:9).

# PROTECTING THE
# FAITH AT HOME

Beloved, while I was very diligent to write to you
concerning our common salvation, I found it necessary
to write to you exhorting you to contend earnestly for the
faith which was once for all delivered to the saints.
—Jude 1:3

At some point, we as fathers have had to stand up, lay down the law, and say no to dangerous things that could harm our family and loved ones. If you've ever had to stand up in this way, then you have followed the example of Jude, who challenged believers to "contend earnestly for the faith" (Jude 1:3). In Jude's day, challenges to this kingdom warrior came from all directions. While outsiders opposed and persecuted the church, false teachers crept into the pews, turning God's grace into license to do as they pleased. Jude was no wimp. He understood and recognized the danger they caused to the church and stood ready to confront them head-on. He challenged his fellow brothers to do the same. The danger is real. Fight! Contend! Do battle! God calls you to stand firm and protect your faith against modern-day enemies. What voices in your own day attempt to drown out sound biblical teaching? Just look at your local television listings. Like Jude, you have the opportunity and responsibility to stand against those things, beginning at home. How can we best prepare for the challenge? Recognize those enemies and their tactics. Do you know how to oppose and defeat them? What stand do you believe God is calling you to take in your own home right now? The challenge is great, but so is the God who is able to keep you from stumbling (Jude 24). Stand fast with one mind! Together let's fight shoulder to shoulder for the faith of the gospel. Sound the alarm! The battle is here. It's time to protect.

## Battle Plan

Contend strongly for biblical faith. Accept no form of alteration (Ephesians 4:14–16; Colossians 2:4–10; 2 Timothy 3:13–17; 2 Peter 3:14–18).

# STANDING OUT IN THE CROWD

So the Lord said, "I will destroy man whom I have created
from the face of the earth, both man and beast, creeping
thing and birds of the air, for I am sorry that I have made
them." But Noah found grace in the eyes of the Lord.
—Genesis 6:7–8

Forces in this world will always try to conform us to their corrupt images. Kingdom warriors find favor with the Lord by choosing to stand out in the crowd. Noah stood out that way. Men around him had become so corrupt that God expressed great sorrow over having ever made them. Their constant sin so offended God that He decided to destroy the world and every living thing. Noah was the exception. His righteous life set him apart in a world made crooked by sin. No doubt Noah found it tempting to conform to the world around him—as we all do—but he remained true to God and His righteous standards. When you build your life on God and live by His standards, you will stand out in a crowd, as a kingdom warrior. This is an everyday battle for the warrior of Christ. You will feel the sting of ridicule and persecution, but you will be in good company!

The Holy Spirit is the key to living under God's grace. This kingdom warrior found favor with God because he desired to live by God's standards. Warrior, do you want to enjoy God's blessings? Live by His rules and standards.

## Battle Plan

Live under the Holy Spirit's control. Avoid ungodliness (Matthew 13:22, Galatians 5:16–18, 6:6–10; 1 Peter 1:13–15; 2 Peter 2:4–11; Hebrews 11:7).

# CONQUERING FEAR

King Artaxerxes said to me, "Why is your face sad, since you
are not sick? This is nothing but sorrow of heart." So I became
dreadfully afraid, and said to the king, "May the king live forever!
Why should my face not be sad, when the city, the place of my
father's tombs, lies waste, and its gates are burned with fire?"
—Nehemiah 2:2–3

In your own life of faith, has God proven trustworthy in all things?
Perhaps the greatest enemy of faith is the fear that takes our attention
away from God and places it on whatever we perceive as a threat.
As a kingdom warrior, you have the faith to overcome your fears
victoriously! Centuries before, Nehemiah faced a similar challenge.
His faith empowered him to look past mistreatment to what God
had called him to do. Nehemiah served the most powerful king of
his time, the Persian ruler Artaxerxes. He had to maintain a sunny
disposition at all times so his personal problems would not disturb
the king. Failure could result in severe consequences, so when the
king asked Nehemiah, "Why are you looking so sad?" this godly
man had every reason to be afraid. Because of his love for God,

Nehemiah spoke his heart and revealed his troubles. The king could have punished him, but instead, he reacted with mercy and practical assistance as he sent Nehemiah to rebuild the walls of Jerusalem. This kingdom warrior made the welfare of God's people a higher priority than his own welfare. Living as a kingdom warrior means making God's priorities our priorities, realizing that they often different from ours. Like Nehemiah, hear your *King* ask you today, "What do you want Me to do for you?" (read Nehemiah 2:4). Take Him at His Word!

**Battle Plan**

Keep your focus on God's goodness and faithfulness, you will find the strength to overcome your fears (Nehemiah 2:1–10; Romans 8:14–17; 2 Timothy 1:6–7; 1 John 4:18–19).

# PLANNING WITH WISDOM

And behold, I propose to build a house for the name of
the Lord my God, as the Lord spoke to my father David,
saying, "Your son, whom I will set on your throne in
your place, he shall build the house for My Name."
—1 Kings 5:5

If you want to accomplish anything significant in any sphere of life, you as a kingdom warrior must do some prayerful planning. Wisdom is the most valuable of assets in the kingdom of God. Many things in life require good planning, a truth the wise king Solomon took into consideration as he prepared to build the Temple in Jerusalem. He was "wiser than all men," and his fame was in all the surrounding nations (1 Kings 4:31). His father, David, was feared by the sword; Solomon, rather, was feared by his wisdom, making him a "wisdom warrior." Solomon had a consuming passion to bring his father's dream of a house of worship for the Lord to completion, but he tempered his passion with careful planning. He realized that rushing into the construction would mean disaster. He sought out construction know-how from his neighbors, did some wheeling and dealing king

Hiram of Tyre to get the building materials, and enlisted a labor crew from around the region. Then he prepared the Temple site. All of Solomon's wise and careful planning paid off greatly. Seven and a half years from the ground-breaking day, this Temple of beauty stood breathtaking on mount Moriah. As men, we need to consciously commit all our plans to the Lord daily. Prayerfully submit your plans to the will of God "right now." As the trusted saying goes, "Wisdom is the principal thing; therefore get wisdom. And in all your getting, get understanding," exhorts Solomon (Proverbs 4:7). Get it?

## Battle Plan

Express continued dependence upon God! Don't presume God's help if it is uninvited (Psalm 37:3–6; Proverbs 16:1–3; James 4:13–16).

# THE RIGHT GUY FOR A TOUGH ASSIGNMENT

One of them, a prophet of their own, said, "Cretans are always liars, evil beasts, lazy gluttons." This testimony is true. Therefore, rebuke them sharply, that they may be sound in the faith."
—Titus 1:12–13

God often calls men of character and commitment to handle His tough assignments in the Kingdom. Only such warriors come prepared to handle them. Among fearless warriors was a young man named Titus, a protégé of another warrior, the apostle Paul. Paul gave to Titus, a young pastor, the tough assignment of setting in order the church at Crete. Crete was a place known for excessive gluttony, cruelty, and lack of discipline. Paul exhorts Titus to exercise his authority by appointing elders, rebuke false teachers, and remove immoral behavior. This was no assignment for the weak of heart! Only a man of strong character who could love God and His Word would be qualified for such a charge. That's a kingdom warrior! Many references to Titus make it clear that he was one of Paul's closet and most trusted companions. Paul spoke of this reliable and gifted companion as his "brother" (2 Corinthians 2:13), his "partner and fellow worker" (2 Corinthians 8:23), and now his "son" (Titus 1:4). How can you be God's man in a tough assignment, whether at home, at work, or at church? Titus walked into this tough assignment and got the job done! If God calls you to handle a tough assignment, He will equip and empower you to get job done as well. Like Titus, you can be eager to depend on God in such assignments. A key part of living as a kingdom warrior is having an eager readiness to do good works! Warriors, are you ready?

## Battle Plan

Recognize that your whole Christian life, from a willingness to do it to actually doing it, is all God's work (Ephesians 6:5–9; Philippians 2:12–18; Colossians 3:22–25; Hebrews 13:20–21).

# A SPARK BECOMES A FIRE

And Peter said to him, "Aeneas, Jesus the Christ heals you.
Arise and make your bed." Then he arose immediately.
—Acts 9:34

People around you need to see God's power working in your life.
You could be the spark that ignites a great spiritual fire! A bedridden
paralytic from the town of Lydda made a discovery that spread far
beyond what he expected or prayed for. Aeneas had no reason to
believe that his miserable lot in life would ever change. After eight
years, he had probably gotten used to living as a beggar. One day,
however, he had an encounter with Jesus through Peter's ministry, as
the apostle traveled from town to town preaching and healing people
in Jesus's name. Peter spent only a few moments with Aeneas, but
those precious seconds totally changed the man's life. After nothing
but a verbal command in Jesus's name, Aeneas suddenly felt his body
grow strong and whole. That wonderful day, Aeneas lived up to the
meaning of his name, "praise"! "The garment of praise for the spirit
of heaviness" (Isaiah 61:3). Aeneas, as kingdom royalty, wrapped
himself with this "kingdom garment" of praise. Any encounter

with Jesus Christ that so radically changes a man will get people's attention. This powerful healing was really designed to bring many to Christ; it was a *fire*! The spark had become a fire (Acts 9:35)! As men, we need to look for ways to focus our attention on the Lord's goodness. God is willing to forgive and restore anyone who comes to Him in faith. Just look at Aeneas's (praise) life! Let's make our lives a life of praise!

**Battle Plan**

Get up! Awake in praise! Humbly ask God to do something great in your life (Psalm 150; Isaiah 61:1–3; Matthew 11:12; Luke 9:1–2; Acts 1:8).

# CONNECT WITH YOUR POWER SOURCE

Now in the morning, having risen a long while
before daylight, Jesus went out and departed to
a solitary place; and there He prayed.
—Mark 1:35

Jesus considered regular prayer vital to His personal well-being and effectiveness in ministry. How much time are you spending with your heavenly Power Source? Daily prayerful intervention helps us serve in our roles as "kingdom warriors." Despite full days of teaching, preaching, doing miracles, and meeting people's needs, Jesus didn't allow anything to get in the way of His prayer times. He kept up an amazingly packed schedule without losing His focus or His energy. How did He manage it? The Gospels reveal that He was energized and empowered through regular times of "pressing in" with His Father. Such prayerful "pressing in" is called intercession. If Jesus, the Son of God and the only perfect man who ever lived, made a priority of connecting with His Father, how much more should we spend time "pressing in" with the One who empowers us to do everything on our plates? God's power alone can change things and bring heaven's rule (kingdom), and the honor and glory for answered prayer are His. However, the praying is ours to do! Jesus's example teaches us the importance of connecting with our heavenly Power Source daily. As men, we must ask for the intervention of His kingdom and obey His voice. Nothing will change unless we pray, press in, intercede, and connect to our Power Source! It proclaims that time alone with our heavenly Father gives us the energy and power we need to accomplish whatever lands on our "to-do" lists. Find yourself a quiet spot and sit down. You might have to bring a cup of coffee. Do you hear Him? He wants you to spend this time of private prayer with Him and Him only. Now, let's pray together.

## Battle Plan

Surrender your life and self-interests in order to gain God's Kingdom goals (Matthew 18:18–19; Luke 11:9–13; John 14:12–14; John 15:1–11).

# RIGHTEOUS IN THE
# MIDDLE OF FILTH

God delivered righteous Lot, who was oppressed by the
filthy conduct of the wicked (for that righteous man,
dwelling among them, tormented his righteous soul from
day to day by seeing and hearing their lawless deeds).
—2 Peter 2:7–8

Godliness results from Jesus Christ living through you by the Holy Spirit. It is not achieved by observing some external code. That's religion! Any attempt to achieve righteousness through a list of external dos and don'ts is fruitless. The Bible calls Lot a "righteous man" even though he lived in the wicked city of Sodom. The only upright man to make his home in the middle of such filth, Lot was tormented over the sin he saw day after day. Righteousness will sometimes trigger negative reactions. So Lot remained alone in suffering the ridicule from people who despised his way of life. Can you imagine how Lot felt? Maybe you can even identify with it. Perhaps you live in a modern-day Sodom. Maybe you're the only godly man working in an environment that lacks any hint of righteousness. Perhaps you feel totally alone in your desire to hold on to a godly life. Take heart, God knows the godly and will deliver you, as He knows the ungodly and will judge them. Though Lot was far from perfect, his love for God keep his mind alert and clear, fit for his walk with God. Grid up the loins of your mind, be sober, and rest your hope fully upon the grace that is to be brought to you at the revelation of Jesus Christ (1 Peter 1:13). "Gird up" signifies readiness for action. In order to have freedom of activity, men in Peter's day would tuck the skirts of their long robes into their belts. Like Lot, you can hold on to righteousness, despite ridicule and be a kingdom warrior "girded" to shine for God in the middle of filth. God will encourage and equip you.

## Battle Plan

Persevere in godliness. Know it is the safest place you can be (Psalm 37; Luke 9:62; Philippians 3:13–14).

# A SPIRIT OF ENCOURAGEMENT

> Then news of these things came to the ears of the church
> in Jerusalem, and they sent out Barnabas to go as far
> as Antioch. When he came and had seen the grace of
> God, he was glad, and encouraged them all that with
> purpose of heart they should continue with the Lord.
> —Acts 11:22–23

Can your friends and loved ones describe you as an encouragement?
The men and women around you need you to be an encouragement.
No one ever gets too much encouragement! Barnabas specialized
in encouragement. His name means "son of encouragement," and it
expresses the kind of warrior he was. In order to encourage you first
need to have "courage" as well. On one of his first missions, Barnabas
persuaded Paul's former victims to accept this violent Pharisee as one
of their own. He convinced these cynical believers that this man has
genuinely converted to faith in Christ (Acts 9:26–28). As a result,
Saul eventually became the apostle Paul. Wow! Later, Barnabas
encouraged Paul as they traveled together on long missionary journeys
(Acts 13 and 14). He invested in a young believer named John Mark,

who struggled at the beginning of his life in ministry (Acts 15:36–39). Barnabas was drawn to those who needed a positive word. The believers in Antioch needed that greatly in order to remain true to the Lord. What made Barnabas such a great source of encouragement? Scripture says that Barnabas was "a good man, full of the Holy Spirit and strong in faith" (read Acts 11:24). Do others see you as a good man, full of the Holy Spirit and strong in faith? If they don't, you can choose now to follow the "Spirit of Encouragement." Let's go!

## Battle Plan

Walk daily in the power of the Holy Spirit so that God can do miracles through you! (Romans 8:13–17; Galatians 5:16–26; Ephesians 5:18–20)

# ACTION BEHIND THE SCENES

Yet I considered it necessary to send to you Epaphroditus,
my brother, fellow worker, and fellow soldier, but your
messenger and the one who ministered to my need.
—Philippians 2:25

Not everyone is called to be a star in the Lord's ministry, but that
doesn't mean what you do for His Kingdom doesn't catch God's eye.
It does! We don't pay enough attention to know the names of the
servants who do the little things that make our ministry successful.
For instance, Joseph made Potiphar look really good because of the
behind-the-scenes labor he did (Genesis 39:4). Before Joshua had
a mega ministry he served behind-the scenes to Moses (Exodus
33:11). Let's not forget before Elisha's name was in lights, his face
was covered by the dust of his rabbi Elijah (1 Kings 19:21). The
same thing is true of men who do the "action behind the scenes" to
make the church function effectively. Consider Epaphroditus, a New
Testament follower of Jesus. His name means "lovely-charming." If
you were to ask most believers today to identify him in scripture, you
might get a reply with a silly look. ("Say who?") Paul considered him

an important part of his ministry because for the work of Christ he risked his life (Philippians 2:30). Epaphroditus was Paul's "fellow warrior" as well as his trusted messenger when the apostle was in prison. Your work is also important to those you have the privilege of serving. In effect, like Epaphroditus, you play a key role in displaying reckless courage as you take "action behind the scenes."

## Battle Plan

Adopt Christ's attitude of servanthood. Aim selflessly for the welfare of others (Matthew 20:26–28; 1 Corinthians 3:5–9, 9:19–23; 12:29–31).

# KEEP IT REAL

Jesus saw Nathanael coming toward Him, and said of
him, "Behold, an Israelite indeed, in whom is no deceit!"
Nathanael said to Him, "How do You know me?" Jesus
answered and said to him, "Before Philip called you,
when you were under the fig tree, I saw you."
—John 1:47–48

The Bible praises men of honesty who tell it like it is. Nathanael,
one of Jesus's disciples, was that kind of man. He didn't worry about
church conventions or camp meetings. When his friend Philip told
him he had met the Messiah, a prophet from Nazareth, Nate replied,
"Nazareth! Can anything good come from Nazareth?" (John 1:46).
*Way to go, Nate!* Philip must have thought. I offer to introduce you
to our Messiah, and you insult His hometown! Nate's words dripped
with skepticism, even sarcasm, but they demonstrated a character trait
that appealed to Jesus, who seemed to genuinely like Nate as soon
as He saw him. Even through the façade of Nathanael's skepticism,
Jesus discerned his transparency of spirit. God blesses you when you
speak to Him and to others with honesty and integrity and when you

are "real" with Him about who you are, what you think, what you struggle with, and what you need. What Jesus liked so much about Nate was his honesty and integrity. Nate may have been a little rough around the edges—we've all been at some point—but with the polish and training Jesus gave him over the next three years, he became a man who made a difference in God's battlefield as a "kingdom warrior." You can too!

**Battle Plan**

Exemplify excellent character and self-control. Don't allow your words to provide an occasion for accusation (Psalm 26:1–3, 32:1–2; John 1:45–51; 1 Timothy 4:12; Titus 2:6–8).

# IT'S ALL ABOUT THE KING

He must increase, but I must decrease.
—John 3:30

To understand the kingdom, we, as kingdom warriors, must understand the *King*. John wrote to lead his readers to a settled faith in Jesus, with the result that they "may have life in His name." John the Baptist was a powerful kingdom warrior. It's hard to imagine such words coming out of this warrior's mouth. Even when given the opportunity, he despised self-advancement. Godly living is living in, through, and for Jesus. John the kingdom warrior attracted big crowds through his powerful preaching, but he remained humble. Instead of pointing to himself as *numero uno*, he pointed to Jesus and said, "He who comes after me ranks higher than I, for He was before me" (John 1:15). For John, it was *all* about the *King*. John avoided the trap of self-glorification. He knew that he was just God's messenger. When a crowd sought to know if John was the *Messiah*, he directed them to Jesus. "ONE mightier than I is coming, whose sandal strap I am not worthy to loose" (Luke 3:16). John's humility was so real that he encouraged his own disciples to follow Jesus. As a husband, father, and brother in Christ, are you a humble person? It is a trait of a kingdom warrior. When given the chance, do you gladly point to Jesus and let Him shine, or do you feel tempted to share the spotlight? Exalt Jesus in your life and service to draw men to Him. Indeed, *He is the King*! It's *all* about *Him*!

## Battle Plan

Don't allow your ministry for Jesus to distract you from your ministry to Him! (John 5:16–23; 6:38, 8:28, 12:2–8; James 4:10)

Printed in the United States
By Bookmasters